Pre Reader
DOUDNA

0509231

14.95

DATE DUE			
APR 0 9 2007			
JUN 2 9 2012			

Tee
Hee

Kelly Doudna

Consulting Editor, Monica Marx, M.A./Reading Specialist

Publishing Company

Published by SandCastle™, an imprint of ABDO Publishing Company, 4940 Viking Drive, Edina, Minnesota 55435.

Printed in the United States.

Credits
Edited by: Pam Price
Curriculum Coordinator: Nancy Tuminelly
Cover and Interior Design and Production: Mighty Media
Photo Credits: Hemera, Image Source, ImageState, PhotoDisc, Stockbyte

Library of Congress Cataloging-in-Publication Data

Doudna, Kelly, 1963-
    Tee hee / Kelly Doudna.
        p. cm. -- (Sound words)
    Includes index.
    Summary: Uses photographs and simple sentences to introduce words for different feelings that sound like what they mean, such as: tee hee, ah-choo, boo hoo, whee, hmm, yuck.
    ISBN 1-59197-452-6
    1. English language--Onomatopoeic words--Juvenile literature. 2. Sounds, Words for--Juvenile literature. [1. English language--Onomatopoeic words. 2. Sounds, Words for.] I. Title.

PE1597.D66 2003
428.1--dc21
                                                                            2003044346

SandCastle™ books are created by a professional team of educators, reading specialists, and content developers around five essential components that include phonemic awareness, phonics, vocabulary, text comprehension, and fluency. All books are written, reviewed, and leveled for guided reading, early intervention reading, and Accelerated Reader® programs and designed for use in shared, guided, and independent reading and writing activities to support a balanced approach to literacy instruction.

Let Us Know

After reading the book, SandCastle would like you to tell us your stories about reading. What is your favorite page? Was there something hard that you needed help with? Share the ups and downs of learning to read. We want to hear from you! To get posted on the ABDO Publishing Company Web site, send us e-mail at:

sandcastle@abdopub.com

SandCastle Level: Transitional

Onomatopoeia
(on-uh-mat-uh-**pee**-uh)
is the use of words that
sound like what they
describe.

These **sound words** are
all around us.

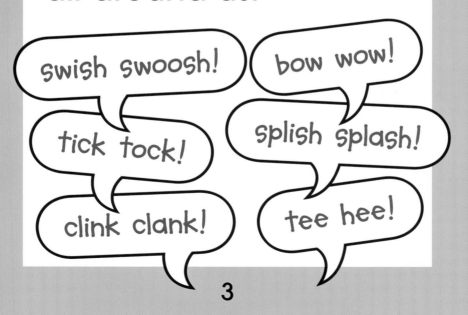

swish swoosh!

bow wow!

tick tock!

splish splash!

clink clank!

tee hee!

Lee laughs at Jill's joke.

Tee hee!

Sandy sneezes.

Ah-choo!

Fran's friend cries.

Boo hoo!

Gail goes down the slide.

Whee!

Wes wonders if the water is warm.

Hmm.

Thad thinks milk is gross.

Yuck!

Pals at Play

Ha ha ha!

Wendy went outside
to play with her friends.

"Ha ha ha!" she laughed.
"This is fun!"

16

Sid slid down the slide.
"Whee!" said Sid.

Sue swung on the swing.

"Woo hoo!" whooped Sue.

18

Mark made a funny face
at Grace.

"Tee hee!" giggled Grace.

Jan jumped out from behind
a tree.

"Eek!" shrieked Eve.

Wendy went home.

"Whew!" she sighed. "I'm tired."

Picture Index

ah-choo, p. 7

boo hoo, p. 9

hmm, p. 13

tee hee, pp. 5, 19

whee, pp. 11, 17

whew, p. 21

22

Glossary

giggle   a silly happy laugh

joke   a funny thing you say to make other people laugh

shriek   a sharp shrill cry

sigh   to let out a deep breath that can be heard, sometimes to express relief or tiredness

About SandCastle™

A professional team of educators, reading specialists, and content developers created the SandCastle™ series to support young readers as they develop reading skills and strategies and increase their general knowledge. The SandCastle™ series has four levels that correspond to early literacy development in young children. The levels are provided to help teachers and parents select the appropriate books for young readers.

Emerging Readers
(no flags)

Beginning Readers
(1 flag)

Transitional Readers
(2 flags)

Fluent Readers
(3 flags)

These levels are meant only as a guide. All levels are subject to change.

To see a complete list of SandCastle™ books and other nonfiction titles from ABDO Publishing Company, visit www.abdopub.com or contact us at:

4940 Viking Drive, Edina, Minnesota 55435 • 1-800-800-1312 • fax: 1-952-831-1632